PLATO IN 90 MINUTES

Paul Strathern

PLATO
(428–348 BC)
in 90 minutes

Constable · London

First published in Great Britain 1996
by Constable and Company Limited
3 The Lanchesters, 162 Fulham Palace Road
London W6 9ER
Copyright © Paul Strathern 1996
The right of Paul Strathern to be identified as author
of this work has been asserted by him
in accordance with the Copyright,
Designs and Patents Act 1988
ISBN 0 09 475950 2
Set in Linotron Sabon by
Rowland Phototypesetting Ltd,
Bury St Edmunds, Suffolk
Printed in Great Britain by
St Edmundsbury Press Ltd,
Bury St Edmunds, Suffolk

A CIP catalogue record of this book
is available from the British Library

All translations are by the author.

Contents

Introduction and background to his ideas

Plato was the ruin of philosophy, or so some modern thinkers would have us believe. According to both Nietzsche and Heidegger, philosophy never recovered from the attentions of Socrates and Plato in the fifth century BC. Philosophy had only been going less than 200 years, and in many ways it had hardly started. But this was where it went wrong, seemingly.

Socrates wrote nothing down, and our main knowledge of him is the quasi-historical character who appears in the dialogues of Plato. It is often difficult to know when this character is putting forward the ideas expressed by the actual Socrates, or simply acting as a mouthpiece for Plato's ideas. But, either way, this figure differed radically from the philosophers who had preceded him. (These are now generally known as the Pre-Socratics.)

So how did Socrates and Plato ruin philosophy before it had properly started? Apparently they made the mistake of treating it as a rational pursuit. The introduction of analysis and cogent argument spoilt the whole thing.

But what was this precious Pre-Socratic tradition that was destroyed by the introduction of reason? The Pre-Socratic philosophers included a number of brilliant oddballs, who asked all kinds of profound questions. 'What is reality?' 'What is existence?' 'What is being?' Many of these questions remain unanswered by philosophers to this day (and this includes those modern philosophers who refuse to play the game by claiming that such questions can't be asked in the first place).

By far the most interesting (and most odd) of the Pre-Socratics was Pythagoras. Today Pythagoras is best remembered for his theorem which equates the squares of the sides of a right-angle triangle to the square of its hypotenuse. For centuries this theorem has provided many with their first genuine mathematical understanding – that they will never understand mathematics. It was Pythagoras who most deeply influenced Plato, and to him we must go for the source of many of Plato's ideas.

Pythagoras was more than just a philosopher. He also managed to combine the roles of religious leader, mathematician, mystic and dietary adviser. This taxing intellectual feat was to leave its mark on his philosophical ideas.

Pythagoras was born on Samos around 580 BC, but fled the local tyranny to set up his religious-philosophical-dietary-mathematical school at the Greek colony of Croton in southern Italy. Here he issued a long list of rules to his pupil-disciple-mystic-gourmets. Amongst other prohibitions, they were expressly forbidden to eat beans or heart, to start first into a loaf of bread or let swallows nest in their roofs – and under no circumstances was one of them to eat his own dog. According to Aristotle, Pythagoras also found time to perform a few miracles – though uncharacteristically Aristotle gives no specific details. In the view of Bertrand Russell, Pythagoras was 'a combination of Einstein and Mrs Eddy' (the founder of Christian Science).

Alas, Pythagoras' impressive range of credentials failed to impress the citizens of Croton. They eventually grew tired of all this, and Pythagoras was forced to flee once more. He settled down the road at Metapontion, where he died around 500 BC. His teachings were to flourish for another hundred years or so, spread all over southern Italy and Greece by his mystic-mathematical disciples. It was in this way that Plato came to hear of Pythagoras.

Like Socrates, Pythagoras took the precaution of writing nothing down. His teachings have only been passed on to us through the works of his disciples. We now know that Pythagoras' disciples were responsible for much of the motley of thought, practice, mathematics, philosophy and bats-in-the-belfry which is today labelled Pythagoreanism. Indeed, Pythagoras' famous theorem concerning the square of the hypotenuse was almost certainly not discovered by Pythagoras himself. (Hearteningly for non-mathematicians, this means that Pythagoras didn't understand Pythagoras' Theorem either.)

Plato was to be deeply influenced by Pythagoras' famous saying: 'All is number.' This is the key to Pythagoras' purely philosophical thinking, which was as profound as it was influential. Pythagoras believed that beyond the jumbled world of appearances there lies an abstract harmonious world of number. In fact, his conception of number was closer to what we would call 'form'. Material objects were not composed of matter, but consisted ultimately of the forms out of which they were created. The ideal world of number (or forms) was filled with harmony, and was more real than the so-called real world. It was Pythagoras, or the Pythagoreans, who discovered the connection between number and musical harmony. In the light of this discovery, Pythagoras' theory of forms (or number) does not seem so far-fetched. Just as it does not seem so far-fetched in the light of modern sub-atomic physics, which readily resorts to number and descriptions of form, rather than definitions of substance.

Such unsubstantial thinking was a frequent characteristic of Pre-Socratic thought. Pythagoras' disciple Heraclitus, for instance, believed that all is flux. He declared: 'No man steps into the same river twice.' Yet curiously, this points away from the purely formal, presaging the thought of another Pre-Socratic, Democritus. It was he who insisted that the universe is made up of atoms. Democritus arrived at this conclusion well over two thousand years before modern scientists decided that perhaps he was right. Philosophers also took a similar length of time to reach the same conclusion as the Ionian Pre-Socratic Xenophanes, who declared candidly: 'No man knows, or ever will know, the truth about the gods and about everything; for even if one happened by chance to say the complete truth, nevertheless one would not know it.' This statement is uncannily similar to the views expressed in the twentieth century by Wittgenstein.

Such was the rich and varied philosophical tradition out of which Plato grew.

Life and work

Plato was a well-known wrestler, and the name by which we know him today was his ring name. Plato means broad or flat: presumably in this case the former meaning, referring to his shoulders. Though some sources insist that this nickname referred to his forehead (again, one presumes the former meaning). At his birth in 428 BC Plato was given the name Aristocles. He was born in Athens, or on the island of Aegina, which lies just twelve miles offshore from Athens in the Saronic gulf. Plato was born into one of the great political families of Athens. His father Ariston was descended from Codrus, the last king of Athens, and his mother was descended from the great Athenian law-maker Solon.

Like any bright member of a political family, Plato's earliest ambitions were in other fields. Twice he carried off the wrestling prize at the Isthmian Games, but seemingly never made it to the Olympics at Olympia. So instead he set about trying to become a great tragic poet, but didn't impress the judges in any of the big competitions. Having failed to win an Olympic gold or become a literary star, Plato was almost resigned to becoming a mere statesman. Then as a last fling he decided to have a go at philosophy, and went off to listen to Socrates.

It was love at first sight. And for the next nine years Plato sat at the feet of his master, absorbing all he could of his ideas. Socrates' combative teaching methods forced his pupil to realize his full intellectual potential, at the same time opening his eyes to the unrealized possibilities of the subject. Yet despite having found his true métier, Plato was still tempted to become a backslider and enter politics. Fortunately he was dissuaded from this aberration by the behaviour of Athenian politicians. When the Thirty Tyrants took over after the Peloponnesian War, two of their leaders (Critias and Charmides) were close relatives. The reign of terror which followed might have inspired a young Stalin or Machiavelli, but it didn't impress Plato. Then the democrats took over. Two years into their rule Plato's beloved teacher was tried on trumped-up charges of impiety and corrupting youth, and sentenced to death. In Plato's eyes, democracy was now tarred with the same brush as tyranny.

Plato's close association with Socrates placed him in a dangerous position, and he was forced to remove himself from Athens for his own good. Thus began his *wanderjahre*, which were to last for the next twelve years. After learning all he could at the feet of his master, he would now learn from the world. But the world wasn't that large in those days, and for the first period of his exile Plato studied just twenty miles down the road in the neighbouring territory of Megara, with his friend Euclid. (This was not the famous geometer, but a former pupil of Socrates who had become renowned for the subtlety of his logic. Euclid had so loved Socrates that he had travelled through enemy Athenian territory disguised as a woman to be present at the death of his master – thus perhaps vindicating his master's earlier stricture that his subtle logical methods were not those of a man.)

Plato stayed with Euclid in Megara for three years, and then journeyed to Cyrene in North Africa to study with the mathematician Theodorus; after this he seems to have travelled on to Egypt. According to one persistent story he now wished to visit some magi in the Levant and ended up travelling east as far as the banks of the Ganges, but this seems unlikely. What we do know is that after over a decade of travelling Plato arrived in Sicily, where he visited the crater of Mount Etna. This was a great tourist attraction of the period – and not just as a geographical phenomenon. Many believed this was what the underworld looked like, and a visit here thus afforded an instructive glimpse of future living conditions. But the crater held an even greater attraction for Plato, owing to its association with Empedocles the fifth-century philosopher-poet. Empedocles had been gifted with such prodigious intellectual powers that he had eventually become convinced he was a god, and had plunged into the boiling lava of Etna to prove it. Though one assumes that by the time of Plato's visit, Empedocles' continuing non-reappearance must have been giving rise to a few doubts on this matter.

More importantly, Plato also made contact with the followers of Pythagoras, who flourished throughout the Greek colonies of Sicily and southern Italy. Pythagoras' discovery of the relation between number and musical harmony had led him to believe that numbers held the key to understanding the universe. Everything could be explained in terms of number, which existed in an abstract realm beyond the everyday world. This theory had a profound effect on Plato, who came to believe that the ultimate reality was abstract. What began as numbers with Pythagoras was to become forms or pure ideas in Plato's philosophy.

The central feature of Plato's philosophy is his Theory of Ideas (or Forms), which he continued to develop all his life. This means that Plato's theory has come down to us in several differing versions, thus giving philosophers sufficient material to argue over for centuries to come. (No philosophical theory can hope to last the pace unless it has room for argument about how it should be interpreted.)

The best explanation of Plato's Theory of Ideas is his own (which is not always the case, in philosophy as elsewhere). Unfortunately Plato's explanation comes in the form of an image, which puts this in the realm of literature rather than philosophy. Briefly, Plato explains that most human beings live as if in a dim cave. We are chained, and facing a blank wall, with a fire at our backs. All we see are flickering shadows playing across the cave wall, and this we take to be reality. Only if we learn to turn away from the wall and the shadows, and escape from the cave, can we hope to see the true light of reality.

In more philosophical terms, Plato believed that everything we perceive around us – the shoes and ships and sealing-wax, and cabbages and kings, of everyday experience – is merely appearance. The true reality is the realm of ideas or forms from which this appearance derives. Thus a particular black horse can be said to derive its appearance from the universal form of a horse and from the ideal of blackness. The physical world we perceive with the senses is in a continual state of change. By contrast, the universal realm of ideas, which is perceived by the mind, is unchanging and eternal. Each form – such as that of roundness, man, colour, beauty and so forth – is like a pattern for the particular objects of the world. But the particular objects are only imperfect, ever-changing copies of these universal ideas. With the rational use of the mind we can refine our notions of these universal ideas, and begin to apprehend them better. In this way we can approach the ultimate reality of daylight which lies beyond the dim cave of our everyday world.

This realm of universal ideas has a hierarchy, leading from lesser forms to more rarefied abstract ideas, the highest of which is the idea of good. When we learn to ignore the world of ever-changing particulars and concentrate on the timeless reality of ideas, our understanding can begin to rise through the hierarchy of ideas to an ultimate mystical apprehension of the ideas of Beauty, Truth and ultimately Goodness.

This leads us to Plato's ethics. By concentrating on the particular world, all we can perceive is apparent good. Only with the help of reason can we gain an insight into the greater universal idea of good. Here Plato is advocating a morality of spiritual enlightenment, rather than any particular rules of conduct. His Theory of Ideas has also been criticized for its lack of practicality. Taking Plato at his word, it has been suggested that all he describes is simply an idea of the world, rather than the world itself. Others claim that Plato's world of ideas exists only in the mind, and has little to do with the world from which these ideas are derived. On the other hand, the essentially transcendental nature of Plato's philosophy meant that much of its thinking was later to become acceptable to Christianity.

Whilst Plato was in Sicily he became a close friend of Dion, the brother-in-law of Dionysius, ruler of Syracuse. Dion took his new friend to meet Dionysius, possibly in the hope of procuring for him an appointment as philosopher-in-residence at the court. But despite Plato's travels through the world he remained very much an aristocratic Athenian, and was not taken with the provincial ways of the Syracusan court. Dionysius was an army officer and a tyrant, who also had inflated literary pretensions. He believed himself to be twice the man of any of his contemporaries. As if to confirm this, he married two women, Doris and Aristomache, on the same day. On his wedding night he had them both in his bed. According to Plutarch, after this he took to spending the night with Doris on the uneven dates in the month, and Aristomache on the even ones. Dionysius appears to have been a man of voracious appetites in all departments, and once held a banquet which lasted ninety days.

Life in Syracuse had quietened down a bit by the time Plato arrived on the scene. In fact it all sounds rather pleasant from Plato's description, even if he 'found nothing to please me in the tastes of a society devoted to Italian cuisine, where happiness was held to consist in stuffing oneself twice a day and never sleeping alone at night'. This was too much stuffing for Plato, whose aristocratic Athenian fastidiousness soon got on Dionysius' nerves.

Dionysius had begun life as a clerk in the civil administration, but had been marked out from the start by his exceptional poetic gifts. He had then risen through the ranks of the army, at the same time tossing off a few verse tragedies of unsurpassed merit (as all his subordinate officers readily agreed). After seizing power Dionysius transformed Syracuse, by a series of brutal conquests, into the most powerful Greek city west of Greece – and in order to smooth diplomatic relations the Athenians made sure that his timeless drama *The Ransom of Hector* was awarded a prize at the Lenaen Festival.

Dionysius was not the kind of man to let himself be cowed by some jumped-up philosophic toff who was trying to cadge a job at his court. When he and Plato turned to discussing philosophy, the sparks soon began to fly. At one point, Plato found himself forced to point out a flaw in Dionysius' thinking.

'You speak like a geriatric fool,' exclaimed Dionysius in disgust.

'And you speak like a tyrant,' replied Plato.

Whereupon Dionysius decided to live up to the philosopher's observation, and had Plato clapped in irons. Plato was placed on a Spartan ship bound for Aegina, where the captain was instructed to sell Plato as a slave. 'Don't worry, he's so much of a philosopher he won't even notice,' remarked Dionysius.

Some sources have maintained that Plato's life was in danger at this point. But the fact that he was sent to Aegina suggests otherwise – as well as indicating that this island was probably his place of birth, rather than Athens. Sending Plato back to his birthplace as a slave was just the kind of humiliation that would have appealed to Dionysius. He could also have been fairly certain that Plato would be recognized and bought by some influential friend – thus avoiding any serious diplomatic repercussions with Athens (which might have prejudiced the judges at the next literary prize-giving).

Dionysius' scheme worked out just as he'd planned. Plato was given a nasty fright (the prospect of having to work for a living was enough to strike a chill in the heart of any true philosopher). And it wasn't long before Plato was spotted in the slave market at Aegina by his well-heeled old friend Anniceris the Cyrenaic, who snapped him up for the bargain price of twenty mina. Anniceris was so pleased with his cut-price philosopher that he sent him back to Athens with enough money to set up a school.

In 386 BC Plato bought a plot of land in the Grove of Academe. This was a mile or so north-west of Athens, beyond the Eriai Gate in the ancient city walls. It was a region of parkland dotted with plane trees, in whose shade stood a number of statues and temples.

And here, amidst the cool avenues and tinkling streams, Plato opened the Academy, gathering around him a group of followers which unusually included several women (amongst whom was Axiothea, who dressed as a man). This is recognized (and recognizable) as the first university.

The Grove of Academe where Plato founded the Academy (and from which the school took its name) was called after a former resident named Hecademus, an obscure semi-divine hero of Attic mythology. Hecademus' main accomplishment appears to have been the planting here of twelve olive trees, offshoots from the sacred olive tree of Athena on the Acropolis. Yet as a result of Plato choosing this site, Hecademus is remembered to this day throughout the civilized world, our version of his name adorning everything from secretarial colleges to cinemas, a Scottish football team, and annual awards for similar semi-divine figures of obscure accomplishment.

Today the Grove of Academe is a long straggly stretch of wasteland in north-western Athens, where the inner suburbs start to grow ragged at the edges. Beneath the trees beside the bus depot lie the odd scattered ancient stones, occasional piles of dumped domestic refuse and benches sprayed with graffiti ('Death Metal', 'Motorbreath'). The site of Plato's Academy, and the house where he lived, are almost certainly lost for ever. But, astonishingly, Hecademus' home is still there. Beneath the archaeologists' protective tin roof you can see its exposed baked mud foundations and the remains of its mud brick walls, which were already almost 2,000 years old by the time Plato set up here.

Meanwhile, just across the wasteland is a modern encampment where conditions comparable to those in Hecademus' pre-historic home still prevail over 4,000 years later. Amidst the cardboard-box dwellings and pools of stagnant water, shaven-headed immigrant children play in the hot sunlight beneath haloes of flies, while their head-scarfed mothers sit bow-legged amongst the refuse suckling naked dark-skinned infants.

'What is Justice?' asks Plato in his best-known work *The Republic*. In this dialogue he assembles Socrates and a cast of characters for dinner at a retired tycoon's mansion. By the time Socrates takes over the conversation, the company has agreed that there's no point in trying to define justice, except in the larger context of society. So Socrates sets about describing his idea of a just society.

The earlier dialogues written by Plato, but starring Socrates, are generally reckoned to contain Socrates' ideas. In the middle and later dialogues these ideas undergo something of a transformation, and here the ideas put forward by Socrates are perceived to be Plato's own. *The Republic* is the finest of the middle-period dialogues, and in the course of his prescription for a just society Plato sets out his ideas on such wide-ranging topics as free speech, feminism, birth-control, public and private ownership and much more. Just the sort of subjects you go out of your way to avoid at any enjoyable dinner party. But *The Republic* wasn't going to be an enjoyable dinner party, we soon discover. And the society it proposed wasn't going to be very enjoyable either. Plato's opinions on the topics mentioned are almost all seriously at odds with the opinions held nowadays by all but earnest bigots and the plain potty.

In Plato's ideal republic there would be no possessions or marriage (except for the lower orders, who were presumably the only people fit for such things). Children would be removed from their mothers soon after birth, and educated communally. In this way they would come to regard the state as their parents, and all their contemporaries would become brothers and sisters. Until the age of twenty these compulsory bastards would be educated in gymnastics and uplifting music. (No Ionian or Lydian music was permitted, only military marches to instil courage and the love of the fatherland.)

All this makes one wonder about Plato's own childhood. And sure enough, we learn from Diogenes Laertius that Plato's father 'made violent love' to his mother, but 'failed to win her'. Although Plato was almost certainly born in wedlock, his mother appears to have soon taken a second husband, and Plato was most probably brought up in a number of households. So perhaps it's no surprise that Plato had little time for family life.

But back to Utopia – according to Plato. At the age of twenty, the dross who had shown insufficient appreciation of their unending regime of physical jerks and brass band music were weeded out. They were then despatched to perform menial tasks – such as becoming farmers or businessmen, and supporting the entire community. Meanwhile the superior students went on to study arithmetic, geometry and astronomy for ten years. Maddened by mathematics, the next batch of failures was despatched to the military. Now only the crème de la crème remained. For five years, until they were thirty-five, they were permitted the great honour of studying philosophy. Then for fifteen years they became involved in the practical study of government, immersing themselves in the ways of the world. And at the age of fifty, they were considered fit to rule.

These philosopher-rulers all lived together in a communal barracks, where they had no private possessions and could sleep together as they chose. There was complete equality of men and women (though in another dialogue Plato does let slip that 'if the soul fails to live well for its appointed time in a man, it passes into the body of a woman'). Living communally and having no personal interests, this élite would thus be above bribery; and their only ambition would be to ensure justice in the state. From amongst this lot was chosen the head of state, the philosopher–king.

Even for the small ideal city-state ('nine miles from the sea') where this was all intended to take place, it would appear to be a recipe for disaster. At best stupefyingly boring – all poets, dramatists, and people who played the wrong type of music were banned (as were lawyers, so you couldn't even sue anyone). And at worst a totalitarian nightmare – quickly developing all the usual unpleasant methods required to keep in place such an unpopular regime.

With hindsight it's easy enough to pick holes in this earnest infantile fantasy. And even Plato's own description involves him in a number of contradictions. Poets were banned, yet Plato himself uses many superb poetic images in the course of his arguments. Likewise worship of the gods, religion and mythology were forbidden, yet Plato includes several myths in this work, and the 'philosopher–rulers' bear an uncanny resemblance to a priestly caste. He also introduces an ideal God of his own, who is implacable and must be obeyed (even though his existence cannot be proved).

In fact, Plato's vision of the ideal republic would seem to be strictly a product of its age. Athens had just been defeated by Sparta in the Peloponnesian War. Neither democracy nor tyranny had worked, and there was a dire need for some kind of government which could provide order. (Indeed, some commentators consider that when Plato speaks of justice, what he often means is something more akin to order.) The answer appeared to lie in a strictly controlled society such as that which prevailed in Sparta. But unlike Athens, Sparta was a philistine, economically backward society, which in order to survive had to produce a caste of mindless hooligans willing to obey any orders and fight to the death. The task of this caste was to inflict terror on the city's increasingly rebellious lower orders, and to cow its increasingly sophisticated and economically powerful neighbours. Plato was either ignorant of this, or unwilling to take it into account.

In an extension of Socrates' naïve ethical belief ('the good are happy'), Plato believed that 'the unjust alone are unhappy'. Impose a just society, and everyone will be fine. But what did he come up with? Just the kind of blueprint you'd expect from an earnest high-minded intellectual closeted in the Grove of Academe. It could never work.

But the astonishing thing is that it *did*. Or something like it did. For over a millennium, medieval society, with its lower orders, its military caste, and its powerful priesthood, bore a remarkable resemblance to Plato's republic. And in more recent times, Communism and Fascism have adopted many of the republic's essential features.

For several years Plato continued to teach at his Academy, establishing it as the finest school in Athens. Then in 367 BC he heard from his friend Dion that Dionysius the tyrant of Syracuse had died, and his son Dionysius (the Younger) had succeeded him.

For years Dionysius the Younger had been kept locked up by his father, in order to thwart any ambitions he might have harboured about premature succession. Incarcerated in the royal palace, Dionysius the Younger had spent his days industriously sawing up pieces of wood, constructing tables and stools.

According to Dion, this was the perfect opportunity for Plato. Here was the ideal ruler for him to instruct in the ways of the philosopher-king. His mind was uncluttered by other ideas (or by any ideas at all, from the sound of it). Now Plato could put his theoretical republic into practice.

For some reason, Plato didn't find this prospect particularly appealing. But in the end 'my fear of losing my self-respect, and becoming in my own eyes a creature of mere words who never put them into practice' forced Plato to succumb to the entreaties of his friend. Twenty years after his first visit, the sixty-one-year-old Plato set out on the long journey to Sicily.

But when Plato arrived he found the court of Dionysius the Younger seething with intrigue. A number of influential courtiers remembered the intellectual toff from his previous visit – and some of them appeared to have it in for Dion, too. Within a few months these enemies of philosophy contrived to have both Plato and Dion accused of treason. (A frequent pitfall for those who scheme to set up a Utopia.) At first the carpenter-king wasn't sure what to do. Then, fearful of Dion's power, he banished his uncle – but refused to allow Plato to leave. He didn't want Plato saying bad things about him when he got back to Athens, he informed the old philosopher.

'I think we have enough subjects to talk about at the Academy, without having to resort to that,' replied Plato.

Fortunately friends soon managed to engineer Plato's escape, and he returned to Athens where his faithful disciples and Dion were waiting for him at the Academy.

But Dionysius the Younger was hurt by Plato's defection. He had very much enjoyed his conversations about philosophy with Plato – even if he had no intention of putting any of his ideas into practice. (Syracuse was hardly in a position to indulge in such experiments. At the time it was the one strong state managing to resist the encroachment of Carthage into Italy. Had an attempt been made to put Plato's republic into practice at Syracuse, this might have completely transformed world history. Though not quite in the way that Plato intended. With the collapse of Syracuse, Carthage would have been free to overrun Italy, crushing the embryo Roman Republic, and Europe could well have spent the next few centuries as part of an African empire.)

Dionysius the Younger seems to have begun to look upon Plato as a kind of father-figure, and he was certainly jealous of Plato's affection for his uncle Dion. The king continued to pester Plato with requests for his return to Syracuse. Distraught, Dionysius declared to all who would listen to him (and these tend to be quite a few when you're king, even if you are tediously distraught for months on end) that his life was no longer worth living without the company of his philosophy instructor. In the end Dionysius sent his fastest trireme to Athens, and threatened to confiscate all Dion's possessions in Syracuse (which were considerable) if Plato didn't come and see him.

Eventually, against his better judgement, the seventy-one-year-old Plato set sail for Syracuse. He appears to have been persuaded by Dion – who might well at this stage have been influenced by concerns other than the possibility of setting up Plato's Utopia and 'demonstrating to the tyrant the primacy of the soul over the body'.

Within no time Plato was once again a virtual prisoner in Syracuse – doubtless twice a day refusing to stuff himself with Italian cuisine, and irritably evicting undesirables from his bed each night. But fortunately Plato was once again rescued, this time with the help of a sympathetic Pythagorean from Taranto, who came to pick him up at dead of night in his trireme. With the galley slaves heaving valiantly beneath the lash, the aged philosopher sped back across the sea towards the safety of Athens. (Some years later Dion was to succeed in what had perhaps been his aim all along. He invaded Syracuse, ousted Dionysius the Younger, and took over himself. So did he attempt to set up Plato's republic, now that he at last had the chance? Apparently not. But poetic justice was to succeed where platonic justice did not. Dion was shortly assassinated – betrayed, curiously enough, by a former disciple of Plato.)

Thus ended Plato's sorties into the political sphere – the Roman Empire was safe. Yet as a result of his untried theories, the medieval world which was to grow out of the Roman Empire would have a model; and later the likes of Stalin and Hitler would have a classical precedent for their endeavours. So was Plato entirely wrongheaded? In his view true knowledge or understanding could only be apprehended by the intellect, and not by the senses. The mind should withdraw from the world of experience if it is to reach the truth. If Plato seriously believed this, it's very difficult to understand why he felt the need to dabble in politics in the first place. Such a philosophic stance is incompatible with the practice of politics. Yet according to Plato: 'Unless philosophers become rulers, or rulers study philosophy, there will be no end to the troubles of men.' (In practice it's turned out precisely the opposite. Rulers inspired by philosophical ideas have caused far more trouble than philosophical ignoramuses.)

The nonpolitical part of Plato's philosophy was also to prove a major influence for many centuries to come. This was largely because it blended well with Christianity, lending what had begun as mere faith a more sound philosophical foundation.

For Plato the human soul consisted of three distinct elements. The rational element strove for wisdom, the active spirit sought conquest and distinction, and the appetites craved gratification. (These elements are echoed in the three elements of society which Plato describes in *The Republic*: the philosophers, the men of action or soldiers, and the dross who merely kept the whole thing going and believed in enjoying themselves.) The righteous man is governed by reason, but all three elements have their part to play. We could not continue without satisfying our appetites, just as the entire state would grind to a halt if the workers gave up working and enjoying themselves, and instead tried to become philosophers. The point is that righteousness can only be achieved when each of the three elements of the soul is fulfilling its own function – much as justice is only achieved in the state when each of the three social elements is fulfilling its own role in society.

By far the most enjoyable of Plato's dialogues is *The Symposium*, which is devoted to a discussion of love in its various manifestations. The Ancient Greeks were not prudish about erotic love, and the section where Alcibiades describes his homosexual love for Socrates ensured that this book was widely suppressed – becoming the original underground classic in the cellars of medieval monasteries. (New editions of *The Symposium* were solemnly placed on the Index of Banned Books by the Catholic Church until 1966.)

In Plato eros is regarded as the soul's impulse towards good. In its lowest form this is expressed in our passion for a beautiful person, and our wish for immortality by producing offspring with that person. (Though it's difficult to see how this applied to Alcibiades – for Socrates was no beauty, and there was no possibility of any offspring here.) A higher form of love involves a union devoted to more spiritual aspirations, giving rise to social good. The highest form of Platonic love is devoted to philosophy, and the pinnacle of this is the achievement of a mystic vision of the idea of the good.

Plato's ideas on love were to have a profound influence. They crop up in the notion of courtly love, so popular with the troubadour poets of the early Middle Ages. Some even see in Plato's understanding of eros an early blueprint for the more lurid sexual fantasies of Freud. Today the notion of Platonic love has been debased to the point where it describes an almost extinct form of attraction between the sexes. Even Plato's Theory of Ideas, intended to lead us to the mystical apprehension of Beauty, Truth and Goodness, has now been stripped of much of its ethereal grandeur. Critics point out that this theory merely supposes the world works like language – with abstract words and concepts assuming the higher ground. This may be a mistaken assumption, but it is one from which we have not yet fully rid ourselves. Plato suggested that the actual world isn't the same as we apprehend and describe it – through experience and language. And why should it be? Indeed, it seems unlikely that it is. But how can we ever tell?

At the age of eighty-one Plato died and was buried in the Academy. Despite the unlikelihood of his philosophy, many of its assumptions still linger in our attitude towards the world. Plato's Academy was to flourish in Athens until it was finally closed down by the

Emperor Justinian in 529 AD, in his attempt to suppress pagan Hellenistic culture in favour of Christianity. This date is now regarded by many historians as marking the end of Greco-Roman culture and the start of the Dark Ages.

Afterword

Just as Socrates was followed by his pupil Plato, so Plato was followed by his pupil Aristotle – thus completing the triumvirate of great Greek philosophers. Aristotle developed and criticized Plato's thought, introducing many of his own ideas, and in the process created a philosophy of his own. However, Plato's philosophy in its purer form continued to flourish at the Academy, where it became known as Platonism.

With the advent of the Roman Empire, this philosophy gradually spread, shedding various aspects of Plato's philosophy on the way. Quite obviously, any discussion of political utopias was unwise in an empire run by the likes of Caligula or Nero. Other ideas, such as those on mathematics, were simply ignored because the Romans weren't interested in mathematics.

Over the years Platonism began to evolve.

A number of its most loyal practitioners eventually came to the conclusion that, although Plato's philosophy was correct, Plato himself often hadn't known what he was talking about. These philosophers decided that *they* knew what Plato was talking about, and the result was a new version of Plato's philosophy known as Neoplatonism. In general the Neoplatonists emphasized the mystical elements of Platonism. They tended to believe in a hierarchy of being, which ascends from multiplicity to the utter simplicity of the Good (or the One).

The chief exponent of Neoplatonism was the third-century AD philosopher Plotinus, who was educated in Alexandria. Plotinus was the pupil of a lapsed Christian who had become a Platonist, and some of Plotinus' ideas were to have an almost Christian tenor. But as Christianity and Neoplatonism spread through the Roman Empire they inevitably came into conflict. For a while, Neoplatonism was seen as the main bulwark against the tide of Christianity.

But the fourth century saw the birth of St Augustine of Hippo, the finest philosophical mind since Aristotle. St Augustine was troubled by the lack of intellectual content in Christianity, and found himself attracted by Neoplatonism. He eventually succeeded in reconciling the philosophy of Plotinus with orthodox Christian theology. In this way Christianity was given a firmer intellectual foundation – and the evolved ideas of Plato were grafted onto the only intellectual force which proved able to survive the ensuing Dark Ages.

Platonism (of one sort or another) thus became part of the Christian tradition, which through the centuries produced a succession of thinkers who understood Plato better than Plato, the Platonists, the Neoplatonists, St Augustine, etc., etc. Platonists continued to flourish in major European universities –

especially in Germany and at Cambridge – until well into the twentieth century, but the species is now thought to be extinct.

Key quotations

Philosophy begins in wonder.

Theaetetus, 155d

Here is a parable which shows how our nature may become enlightened or remain unenlightened. Imagine the condition of men as living in a sort of underground cavern, with a long entrance open to the light. Here men have existed since childhood, fettered by the leg and the neck, so that they cannot move or turn their heads in any way, and can only see in front of them. Higher up, and some distance behind them, is the light of a burning fire; and between the fire and the prisoners is a path with a parapet along it, like the screen at a puppet show which conceals the performers while they display their puppets above it.

I can picture it, he replied.

Now behind the parapet imagine there are men carrying all kinds of objects – including figures of men and animals, in stone and wood and various other materials – which project above the parapet. Some of these people would be speaking, and some would be silent.

This is a strange image you conjure up, he said, and those chained men are strange prisoners.

No, they are just like us, I replied. For, to begin with, do you think such prisoners would see anything of themselves, or of one another, except for the shadows cast by the firelight onto the wall of the cave facing them?

How could they see more, if their heads are prevented from turning?

And they would see just as little of the objects being carried past.

Of course.

Now, if they were able to talk to one

another, surely they would suppose that in naming the shadows they saw they were in fact naming the actual objects?

Certainly.

And if their prison had an echo from the wall facing them, when one of the passers-by behind them spoke the prisoners would naturally assume this came from the shadow passing before their eyes.

By Zeus, they would indeed, he said.

In all ways, then, the prisoners would consider reality to be nothing else than the shadows of those artificial objects.

Inevitably, he agreed.

The Republic, Book VII, 514a–c

We must then conclude that education is not, as some claim, the introducing into a soul of knowledge which was not there beforehand – as if they were introducing sight into a blind eye.

That is what they say it is.

But our argument shows that the capacity for understanding truth is innate in each man's soul, and that the way in which he learns is like an eye which cannot be turned from the darkness towards the light except by turning the whole body. In the same way the entire soul must be turned away from this world of change and shadows until its eye is able to endure the bright shining light of reality, and the brightest of all realities, which we have called the Good.

The Republic, Book VII, 518b–c

God is blameless.

The Republic, Book X, 617e

Do not forget that popular favour is a way to achievement, whereas an arbitrary temper has solitude for company.

Letters, IV, 321c

A man is just in the same way that a state is just. And we mustn't forget that justice in the state means that each of the three classes found within it is performing its proper function ... each of us is just and does his duty only when each part of us performs its proper function ...

The Republic, Book IV, 441d (c in some translations)

It is the business of reason to rule, exercising wisdom and foresight on behalf of the entire soul, while the spirited element should act as its subordinate and ally ...

When these two elements have been reared and trained to understand their own true functions, they should be set to rule over the mass of our appetites, which make up by far the largest part of our soul, and are by nature insatiable. These ever-demanding appetites must be watched over with constant vigilance, so as to prevent them from gorging themselves on the so-called pleasures of the body, and thus becoming so huge and insatiable that the body no longer fulfils its proper role but instead attempts to overturn and enslave the entire life of man.

The Republic, Book IV, 441e & 442a

I had a dream, and in this dream I was told that the first elements out of which all things including you and I are made, are such that no one can give an explanation of them. Each of them by itself can only be named; we cannot attribute anything further to them. We cannot even say that they exist, or that they do not exist, if we mean to speak of them alone, for to do so would be to imply the attributes of existence or non-existence . . .

We cannot define any of these primeval elements. They can only be named, for they have nothing but a name. Yet the things composed of these elements, because they are thus complex, they are defined by a combination of names which makes up a description, for a description is the essence of their definition.

Theaetetus, 201e (b in some translations) & 202b

Suppose that when someone sees or hears or notices something he says to himself: 'What I perceive looks rather like something else, though it is in fact only a poor imitation'. Don't you agree that the person who receives this impression must have had previous knowledge of that 'something else', and is in fact being reminded of it?

Of course . . .

Then we must have had some earlier knowledge of equality before we first saw things which were almost equal, without being fully so.

I agree.

And at the same time we agree that we didn't and couldn't have come by this notion of equality except by sight or touch or one of the senses. I am treating them as all being the same.

They are, Socrates, for the purposes of our argument.

So it must be by the senses that we become aware of the notion that things which are almost equal are not absolutely equal. Yet we must have a notion of this absolute equality, or there would be no standard with which to compare the things that we perceive as being almost equal.

That sounds logical enough, Socrates.

But surely we first see and hear and use our senses only at birth?

Of course.

But previously we agreed that we must have knowledge of equivalence and non-equivalence before we use our senses, or we wouldn't be able to make any sense of them.

Yes.

Which means we must have had this knowledge before we were born.

So it appears.

Therefore, if we had this knowledge before we were born, and knew it when we were born, this means we had knowledge not only of equality and relative equivalence, but also of all absolute standards. And this same argument which we applied to absolute equality, applies just as much to the absolutes of beauty, goodness, morality, and holiness. And also, I maintain, to all those characteristics to which we apply the term 'absolute'. This shows that we must obtain knowledge of such absolutes before we were born.

Phaedo, 73c & 74e (end) *et seq*.

It is said that Socrates had a dream about a cygnet, which sat on his knees. It quickly grew plumage and became a swan, then flew off letting out a loud sweet cry. Next day Plato was introduced to Socrates as a pupil, and Socrates immediately recognized him as the swan in his dream.

Diogenes Laertius, *Lives of the Eminent Philosophers*, Book 3, 5

Chronology of significant philosophical dates

6th century BC	The start of western philosophy with Thales of Miletus.
end of 6th century BC	Death of Pythagoras.
399 BC	Socrates sentenced to death in Athens.
c387 BC	Plato founds the Academy in Athens, the first university.
335 BC	Aristotle founds the Lyceum in Athens, rival school to the Academy.
324 AD	Emperor Constantine moves capital of Roman Empire to Byzantium.
400 AD	St Augustine writes his

	Confessions. Philosophy absorbed into Christian theology.
410 AD	Sack of Rome by Visigoths.
529 AD	Closure of Academy in Athens by Emperor Justinian marks end of Greco-Roman era and start of Dark Ages.
mid 13th Century	Thomas Aquinas writes his commentaries on Aristotle. Era of Scholasticism.
1453	Fall of Byzantium to Turks, end of Byzantine Empire.
1492	Columbus reaches America. Renaissance in Florence and revival of interest in Greek learning.
1543	Copernicus publishes *De revolutionibus orbium caelestium* (*On the Revolution of the Celestial Orbs*) proving

mathematically that the earth revolves around the sun.

1633   Galileo forced by Church to recant heliocentric theory of the universe.

1641   Descartes publishes his *Meditations*, the start of modern philosophy.

1677   Death of Spinoza allows publication of his *Ethics*.

1687   Newton publishes *Principia*, introducing concept of gravity.

1689   Locke publishes *Essay Concerning Human Understanding*. Start of Empiricism.

1710   Berkeley publishes *Principles of Human Knowledge*, advancing Empiricism to new extremes.

1716	Death of Leibnitz.
1739–40	Hume publishes *Treatise of Human Nature*, taking Empiricism to its logical limits.
1781	Kant, woken from his 'dogmatic slumbers' by Hume, publishes *Critique of Pure Reason*. Great era of German metaphysics begins.
1807	Hegel publishes *The Phenomenology of Mind*: high point of German metaphysics.
1818	Schopenhauer publishes *The World as Will and Representation*, introducing Indian philosophy into German metaphysics.
1889	Nietzsche, having declared 'God is dead', succumbs to madness in Turin.
1921	Wittgenstein publishes

Tractatus-Logico-Philosophicus, claiming the 'final solution' to the problems of philosophy.

1920s   Vienna Circle propound Logical Positivism.

1927   Heidegger publishes *Sein und Zeit* (*Being and Time*), heralding split between analytical and continental philosophy.

1943   Sartre publishes *L'être et le néant* (*Being and Nothingness*), advancing Heidegger's thought and instigating Existentialism.

1953   Posthumous publication of Wittgenstein's *Philosophical Investigations*. High era of Linguistic Analysis.